©1976 CARNEGIE-MELLON UNIVERSITY

Library of Congress Catalog Card Number 76-14369
ISBN Number 0-915604-05-1

Collective Bargaining

Labor Relations in Steel: Then and Now

I. W. Abel

Distributed by Columbia University Press
New York — Guildford, Surrey

The Benjamin F. Fairless Memorial Lectures endowment fund has been established at Carnegie-Mellon University to support an annual series of lectures. An internationally known figure from the world of business, government, or education is invited each year to present three lectures at Carnegie-Mellon under the auspices of its Graduate School of Industrial Administration. In general, the lectures will be concerned with some aspects of business or public administration; the relationships between business and government, management and labor; or a subject related to the themes of preserving economic freedom, human liberty, and the strengthening of individual enterprise—all of which were matters of deep concern to Mr. Fairless throughout his career.

Mr. Fairless was president of United States Steel Corporation for fifteen years, and chairman of the board from 1952 until his retirement in 1955. A friend of Carnegie-Mellon University for many years, he served on the board of trustees from 1952 until his death. In 1959 he was named honorary chairman of the board. He was also a leader and co-chairman of Carnegie-Mellon's first development program, from its beginning in 1957.

Mr. I.W. Abel, President of the United Steelworkers of America, was born in Magnolia, Ohio. His father was a blacksmith of German ancestry; his mother was descended from Welsh coal miners.

In 1925, Mr. Abel went to work for the American Sheet and Tin Mill Works in Canton, now a subsidiary of the U.S. Steel Corporation, and learned the molding trade. Later he worked for the Canton Malleable Iron Company and the Timken Roller Bearing Company.

In 1930, as a victim of the Depression, he lost his job at Timken. The times were so bad that he felt fortunate in finding a job firing kilns in a brickyard for 16 cents an hour, 12 hours a day, 7 days a week. Mr. Abel later recalled: "It was that job more than any other that helped to develop my social thinking." The Depression taught him that a strong labor movement was necessary to protect workers and give them dignity and security.

In 1936, Mr. Abel volunteered his services to the Steel Workers Organizing Committee, forerunner of the United Steelworkers of America. He helped organize Local Union 1123 at the Timken plant and served successively as its financial secretary, vice president and president.

In 1937, the late Philip Murray, founding president of the Steel Workers Organizing Committee, and of its successor the United Steelworkers, chose Mr. Abel for a staff position with the Steel Workers Organizing Committee. (That was the year of the "Little Steel Strike." Although Mr. Abel's local union was not involved, he walked the picket lines and helped rally financial support for the strikers).

In 1942, Mr. Murray appointed Mr. Abel to head the Union's newly-created District 27 with headquarters in Canton. Subsequently, he was elected Director of that District.

Ten years later, Mr. Abel was the unanimous choice for the office of International Secretary-Treasurer. In 1965 he was elected International President, and was re-elected for four-year terms in 1969 and 1973.

seven

INTRODUCTION

At the outset I want to express my personal appreciation for the invitation to deliver this series of lectures. This is both an honor for me and the organization I have been privileged to serve for most of my working adult life — the United Steelworkers of America.

It is my hope that the three lectures will impart an understanding of the sacrifice, heroism, grit, dedication and perseverance required from so many, over a long period of time, to establish and build the United Steelworkers of America. Also I hope to be able to demonstrate the positive role that organized labor plays in our free society. And finally, I will discuss the growth and development of the more mature relations that exist today between our Union and industrial management.

Carnegie-Mellon occupies a unique and respected place on the American educational scene. As I prepared these lectures it struck me that in some ways Carnegie-Mellon University's changing educational outlook — from the days of its founding by Andrew Carnegie in 1900 until today — parallels the transformation of labor-management relations in our society.

At the turn of the century the University reflected the philosophy of its founder; to wit, labor unions were an invasion of property rights, if not downright subversive, and had to be crushed. I'm glad that view has changed at CMU and doubt I'd be here if it hadn't.

Today CMU recognizes that trade unions are not only here to stay but are an integral part of the economic process and make a socially useful contribution to our American way of life. This demonstrates that even universities can learn. I hope I'm not unmasking him when I note how pleased I was to discover that the dean of your school of business, Dr. Arnold Weber, has a labor background.

Deserving of praise here are courses such as the one on Industrial Relations where business students, in order to gain practical experience, negotiate contracts with representatives of labor including some from our own Steelworkers Union. I must acknowledge a prejudice about whom I want to come out on top in these negotiations, and I can't help bragging that we have not done too badly. While these negotiations are only practice, I'm interested in them, because practice makes perfect. And while labor-management interests overlap in some important areas, they are not synonymous. So I hope the students aren't learning too many of our collective bargaining techniques and tricks.

On a more profound level I think it is good that students, who will be the business leaders of tomorrow, come to have, I am told, greater human and economic respect for steelworkers who may not have had the advantages of a university education. The students learn that working people can hold their own because they have gained a wealth of knowledge in the tough school of industrial struggle and life.

That students became aware of this through participation in such courses is good for business and labor but, more importantly, good for our Nation's democratic system. A course such as this given at CMU reflects a constructive outlook on labor-management affairs. While those on opposite sides of the bargaining table will certainly not agree on every issue, there is much that they can learn from each other. This helps to reduce disagreements based on misunderstandings and, in areas where there are real clashes of interests, it helps produce constructive compromise. Any program that brings students and trade unionists together, I think, is educationally sound and economically and socially valid. I hope that other universities will adopt such courses.

In my first lecture I will concentrate on the pre-union days of Steelworkers and the tremendous obstacles that the men of the mills had to surmount in order to build their union. The second lecture will demonstrate the constructive role of organized labor in our democratic society, and the final lecture will describe the dramatic and mutually beneficial change that has occurred in the relationship between our Union and the major Basic Steel companies. Each of the presentations are interrelated. The first two lay the groundwork for my final lecture which, hopefully, will demonstrate how far we've come. The first part of the story — this first lecture — is largely one of struggle and sacrifice.

1975

Collective Bargaining
Labor Relations in Steel:
Then and Now

eleven

Collective Bargaining

Labor Relations in Steel:
Then and Now

I. The Steelworkers:
From Defeats to Survival to Growth

I. The Steelworkers:
From Defeats to Survival to Growth

The men who labored in the steel mills in the early, unorganized days of the industry could be said to exist — not live; exist — in a state of industrial slavery. It was the end of the 19th century and the beginning of the 20th century in America but for the workers it was still the Dark Ages. Those early workers did not belong to a union but they paid their dues in the form of blood, limb and life itself. Their bodies bent under the weight of a 12-hour day, the seven-day week. They became "old" at 40. Only the hardiest could survive the long hours, the miserable conditions. The work was dangerous and dirty. In one year, 127 Eastern Europeans died on the job in the steel mills of Allegheny County.

I came across a most revealing bit of information about the tremendous contrast in income for the rich of America and the working poor of America in 1900. It was in a book, *The Big Change,* by Frederick Lewis Allen, published by Bantam books in 1961. The writer noted that Andrew Carnegie, in 1900, owned 58½% of the stock of his steel company. That year it made a profit of $40 million. Carnegie's personal gain, the author pointed out, whether or not he took it in dividends, was well over $23 million *and* he didn't have to pay any income taxes. During 1896-1900 he averaged an annual income of $10 million. At the time that Carnegie was enjoying this tax-free income in the millions, the average annual wage of American workers was somewhere around $400 or $500, according to a fairly objective calculation. Carnegie's annual income then was at least 20,000 times greater than that of the average workman.

The common feeling about America in those days was that everybody could get rich quick. In fact, many of the early workers were immigrants, induced to come by "get-rich-quick" promises. But their letters back home urged others not to come to America because they were — in the words of one worker — "too weak for America." Others wrote, "In America one must work for three horses."

Job security was a stranger to these workers. An English visitor observed in 1901 that the American practice was to get rid "of any man, however exalted his position, when there is the least evidence that his efficiency and his power of endurance are waning."

Management was unconcerned with the steelworker as a human being. The early steelworkers received less consideration than the tools and machinery with which they worked. Tools and machines were expensive to replace; new workers cost nothing. "As humanitarians, we might regret harmful overwork," observed a noted metallurgist, H. M. Howe, in 1890, but he added, "as managers. . .we would not be justified in diminishing our employers' profits."

The American Steel Industry of that era was determined to produce steel at the lowest possible cost, and most of the pressure for economizing focused on labor costs and at the worker's expense. By more than coincidence, gang foremen in those days were called "pushers." An English visitor, returning from a look at American steel production methods, commented, "The bosses drive the men to an extent that the employers would never dream of attempting in this country."

That was the work pattern: Maximum physical labor at inhumanely long hours.

Long hours was the established pattern for as long back as steel men could recall. Keepers in Ohio blast furnaces in 1882 averaged 77 hours a week; laborers 64 hours. In 1910, for the entire country, keepers worked 83.9 hours, and laborers 72.6 hours. An extensive Federal investigation in 1910 found that the standard shift was 12 hours. In an investigation of complaints against Bethlehem Steel in South Bethlehem, Federal investigators found a 12-hour day, a seven-day week, speed-up, numerous accidents and a wage too low to support the family of an unskilled worker.

In 1912, Percival Roberts, a director of Carnegie-Illinois Steel Corp., was testifying before a Congressional investigating committee, and was asked to explain the excessive hours prevailing in the Steel Industry. This was his answer: "Who shall say (what) is the proper limit? There is no doubt that the minimum number. . .is the pleasantest; but, in the economies of the world, how shall we determine what that limit might be?"

The Pittsburgh Associated Charities in 1910 found that a steelworker, working 12 hours a day every day of the year, still could not provide his family of five the barest necessities of life.

In 1901, the average hourly rate for common labor in 49 steel plants was 13.7 cents an hour. By 1910 it had painfully inched up to 16.1 cents an hour, or the magnificent sum of $1.93 for a 12-hour day. One *half* of all steelworkers in 1910 earned under 18 cents an hour; one-fifth of the work force received 16 cents an hour; the semi-skilled received between 18 cents and 25 cents an hour. Skilled workers did better than that but only 5% of the skilled workers were paid more than 50 cents an hour.

When steel's Charles Schwab appeared before a Congressional committee in 1912 he was asked about wages of steelworkers. Representative A. O. Stanley cited figures that showed that Pennsylvania furnace workers had raised their output by 58% from 1902 to 1909 while their wages had risen only 10%. Congressman Stanley wanted to know why their wages had risen only 10%. Could not the workers' earnings have increased much more without eliminating profits? Yes, Schwab answered, but "it would be bad manufacturing, I can tell you."

The living conditions were as intolerable as working conditions. Workers lived in crowded houses, without toilets and with poor ventilation. In Sharpsburg, Pennsylvania, an Italian family and nine boarders existed without running water or a toilet in four rooms on the third floor of a ramshackle tenement.

This, then, is a brief but factual account of how the early steelworker lived. He was subjected to long, back-breaking physical labor. His pitifully inadequate wages denied him even a minimum of security and dignity amid some of the most depressing living conditions found in America at the time.

In the dawn of steel-making in America there also prevailed a ruthless, unrelenting and naked anti-union policy on the part of the steel companies. It continued right through the thirties when these union-busting tactics were experienced by many of us who are today still active in our Union.

Early attempts to organize workers in the Basic Steel Industry were no match for the power and influence of the steel companies. The Amalgamated Association of Iron, Steel and Tin Workers, a union based on the principle of uniting employees by their crafts, did organize several plants in the Pittsburgh district — including Jones & Laughlin Steel and a company in Homestead owned by Andrew Carnegie. But the Amalgamated was a weak union, handicapped by its policy of catering only to skilled craft workers. Moreover, it lacked numerical and financial strength.

In 1892 — a year etched in the minds of steelworkers — Carnegie decided to cut wages. The Amalgamated union members struck in protest. The manager of the Homestead works — Henry C. Frick — put in charge by Carnegie when he departed for Scotland, handed the workers an ultimatum: accept the company's proposal by June 24, or no further negotiations would be held.

A meeting with the company on June 23 produced no agreement, and Frick closed down the plant on July 1. He also announced the plant would reopen on July 6 with non-union workers.

To enforce this he tried to bring in 300 Pinkerton agency guards by moving them up the Monongahela River on barges. But the strikers got wind of this and staged a mass confrontation. On the morning of July 6, 1892, the striking workers and the Pinkertons clashed. When the battle was over, seven strikers and three Pinkertons were dead and many others wounded.

Troops were called in, strikebreakers poured into the plant, and the union was beaten. Following the Homestead

seventeen

strike, Frick wrote to Carnegie: "We had to teach our employees a lesson, and we have taught them one that they will never forget." Carnegie Steel announced publicly that it would never again recognize a labor organization. One of the lessons of these two statements is that it never pays to say "never."

After Homestead it was all downhill for the Amalgamated Association. By 1910 it had workers under contract in only one small open hearth plant. Organization of the Steel Industry had been thwarted. The workers had only one right remaining. "If a man is dissatisfied," said President F. N. Hoffstot of the Pressed Steel Car Co., "it is his privilege to quit."

It wasn't until after World War I that another serious effort was made to organize the Basic Steel Industry. Meanwhile, working conditions had remained the same: Long hours, dangerous work, an unbending anti-union, open-shop policy, use of plant spies to spot potential trouble-makers, use of the blacklist and outright discharge.

The industry's approach was an over-powering paternalism. Management went to great lengths to show concern for workers in every way except through decent wages and shorter hours. Company officials made a fetish of supporting local YMCA's, building playgrounds, offering stock purchase plans, displaying concern over injuries on the job, establishing company libraries and planting gardens to brighten up plant areas. The companies encouraged workers to purchase homes and some offered low-interest mortgage money. Others built company houses and rented them to workers at bargain rates. The purpose was to strengthen the attachment of the worker to his community, increase his dependence on the company and to reduce the danger of his leaving for other work. It was also an attempt to persuade the workers that they, indeed, were well treated.

Ironically, the short-sighted labor relations policies of management — low wages and job insecurity — at that time provided the companies with a work force made up largely of demoralized itinerants who drifted from job to job in search of better conditions which constantly eluded them. These kind of workers, the companies found, were unproductive and unreliable. It was in desperation, then, that the companies turned to paternalistic measures they believed would satisfy and stabilize their work force.

One practitioner of that day gave us a frank and revealing explanation of paternalism: Judge Gary told a group of his peers at a dinner at the Waldorf that "The man who has the intelligence and the success and the capital to employ labor has placed upon himself voluntarily a responsibility with reference to his men. We have the advantage of them in education, in experience, in wealth, in many ways, and we must make it absolutely certain that under all circumstances that we treat them right." The remark was greeted with applause, according to the record. Judge Gary also commented, "Considering their education and experience, our men have been very decent in their conduct toward us."

After World War I, another unsuccessful effort to organize the steelworkers took place. War had heightened a sense of sacrifice and the workers responded with record production. Hours had lengthened by 1919 to 82 hours a week for laborers. Living conditions deteriorated. The workers did not think they deserved such conditions after their unselfish contributions to the war effort and it was thought the time was ripe for union organization.

Fifteen international unions of the American Federation of Labor jointly launched a steel organizing drive that again was doomed to failure. A major problem this time was the jurisdictional disputes that broke out among the 15 unions, all of which claimed as members certain steelworkers, generally depending upon their special crafts or skills. Once more it became clear that steelworkers could not be organized along craft lines.

Opposition to the 1919 steel organizing drive was as strong and ruthless as ever. The mayor of McKeesport refused permits for meetings. No halls could be rented for union meetings in Homestead, Braddock or Monessen. Union organizers were stopped and arrested at railroad stations by Pinkerton detectives in Aliquippa and other steel towns. But a head of steam had been built up and the men decided to strike.

Two days before the strike, the sheriff of Allegheny County banned outdoor meetings throughout the county. On a Sunday afternoon state troopers, wielding clubs, broke up a peaceful gathering of workers in Clairton and arrested many for inciting a riot. The companies and the press played up the radical background of one of the organizers, and the Red Scare was used with effectiveness.

The strike was doomed. Company repression, the open use of strikebreakers, a weakening morale among union members and patriotic propaganda all had their effects on the workers. On January 8, 1920, the unions announced that the steel companies had by "arbitrary and ruthless misuse of power" crushed the latest attempt to organize steelworkers.

Once again the Steel Industry reigned supreme. The intolerable conditions, with the exception of the 12-hour day, existing before World War I were to be continued through the 1920's. Public pressure forced the steel companies to go to the eight-hour day in 1923 but with a corresponding cut in earnings. Otherwise, Steel Industry officials were serenely confident that their latest victory over the union would reward them with a subservient, permanently non-union labor force. But looming on the horizon was the Great Depression that would level the scales of justice for workers. The companies simply could not foresee the Wagner Act that would provide Federal protection for the workers' right to organize and bargain collectively, or the militancy of John L. Lewis and his relentless crusade for industrial unionism.

The idea of organizing mass production workers on an industry-wide basis into one union instead of by craft into several unions was championed by Mr. Lewis, president of the AFL United Mine Workers who gave birth to the CIO — the Committee for Industrial Organization. The coal miners and a few other unions in the clothing trades and elsewhere already were organized on an industrial union basis. Now under Lewis' leadership the steelworkers, auto workers, rubber workers and other workers in the Nation's great manufacturing industries, long insulated and isolated from union organization, burst into union fever. Still the AFL continued to sternly resist the growth of the industrial union concept and this led to a major split in organized labor. The AFL, in 1935, expelled six unions that had helped form the CIO and the fight was on.

In 1936, the Steel Workers Organizing Committee — SWOC — was formed and initially financed by John L. Lewis and the Miners' Union with a loan of $500,000. The drive which — at long last — would organize the steel mills got underway with the approval of all remaining lodges of the old Amalgamated Association.

The men who were to lead the organizing drive met on June 17, 1936, in downtown Pittsburgh. The chairman of SWOC was Philip Murray, a seasoned union man who learned about worker exploitation in his native Scotland where he mined coal at the age of 10. He came to the United States at the age of 16 and again went to work in the coal mines. Mr. Murray, a born leader, rose to International Vice President of the United Mine Workers and later was to become the founder and first president of the United Steelworkers of America. Also at that first meeting of SWOC was Secretary-Treasurer David J. McDonald, and Vice Presidents Van A. Bittner and Clinton S. Golden. These four men, more than any others, were a lasting influence on all steelworkers in the United States and Canada.

The CIO provided 150 experienced organizers to SWOC, and the drive started with a meeting on June 21, 1936 in McKeesport, Pennsylvania. Because the companies again refused to okay a meeting place, a coal truck served as the platform for union speakers on the banks of the Youghiogheny River. After that historic beginning, organizers were sent into vital steel areas throughout the country. Meanwhile the industry was again girding for a union war.

Once more the industry would resort to strikebreaking, industrial espionage and private police systems, along with

twenty-one

something new — an arsenal of industrial munitions.

As a Congressional committee — the LaFollette Committee — was to reveal years later, it found, and I quote from the Committee's report: "that the purchasing and storing of 'arsenals' of firearms and tear and sickening gas weapons is a common practice of large employers of labor who refuse to bargain collectively with legitimate labor unions and that there exists a large business of supplying gas weapons to industry."

In fact, the LaFollette Committee found that the corporations bought more tear and sickening gas than did law enforcement agencies, and that Republic Steel "bought four times as much as the largest law enforcement purchaser." The Committee listed these purchases of gas munitions: Republic Steel, $79,712.42; United States Steel, $62, 028.12; Bethlehem Steel, $36,173.69; Youngstown Sheet and Tube, $28,385.39; and National Steel, $12,085.37. "The principle purpose of such weapons," the Committee stated, "is aggression. Their use results in violence, embitters industrial relations and hampers peaceful settlement of industrial disputes." The Committee made its report after the brutal "Little Steel Strike" of 1937.

Despite all-out company resistance, this time things would turn out differently. The defeats of the past were to be erased by the victories of the present and the future.

At the end of 1936, SWOC Chairman Murray announced that a record 125,000 steelworkers had joined the union and that 154 local union lodges had been established. And in 1937, the SWOC reached an historic milestone in labor history and the history of the union. That was the year that Carnegie-Illinois — now known as U.S. Steel, the Steel Industry's giant — recognized the inevitable, by recognizing the union.

On March 2, 1937, it was announced that the company had signed an agreement with SWOC. The contract provided minimum wages of $5 a day, established the 40-hour week, included some safety and health measures, called for a one-week paid vacation and established July 4, Labor Day and Christmas as paid holidays. And, most importantly, a system for settling grievances was set up.

That agreement with a major steel company broke the dam. By the first week in May, 1937, there were 110 steel firms under union contract. Yet, some strong citadels of resistance still faced SWOC, and before 1937 had run its course, more lives were to be lost and the ugly side of some companies' anti-union tactics was to surface once again.

The citadels of resistance were a combination of so-called "Little Steel" companies — Bethlehem, Republic, Inland and Youngstown Sheet and Tube. They refused to recognize the union and rebuffed every effort to negotiate. Their workers, in late Spring 1937, finally were forced to strike.

The strike stretched over seven states. A thousand workers demonstrated their determination to win this strike during a Memorial Day parade and meeting in a field near the Republic Steel plant in Chicago. It was a peaceful gathering and a holiday spirit prevailed. Chicago police confronted the paraders with drawn clubs and hands on revolvers. The workers were ordered to disperse and a moment later, on signal, the police attacked the workers with bullets, clubs and tear gas. Ten marchers were killed by gunfire. Seven were shot in the back, three in the side and none in the front. Thirty others, including one woman and three children, were wounded with gunfire; 28 others were beaten so badly they required hospitalization. The incident is known as the 1937 "Memorial Day Massacre," and rightfully so. It is a sad footnote in labor history. A newsreel film of this "Massacre" was so shocking it was suppressed but was later subpoenaed by the LaFollette Committee.

In addition to those killed on Memorial Day in Chicago, six other SWOC members lost their lives on picket lines during this bitter strike. Three were killed in Massillon, Ohio, two died in Youngstown, Ohio, and one was fatally injured by a tear gas projectile at Beaver Falls, Pennsylvania.

LaFollette Committee hearings later disclosed that the four steel companies and authorities in states, counties and

twenty-three

municipalities affected by the strike spent more than $178,000 for all types of munitions, including machine guns, submachine guns, army rifles, pistols, revolvers and large quantities of gas. The Committee also uncovered a widespread practice of employers furnishing munitions to law-enforcement agencies during strikes. For example, it found that Bethlehem Steel had paid for stockpiling gas equipment for the police of Johnstown, Pennsylvania, where one of the struck plants of the company was located.

Later, the National Labor Relations Board, in 1938, reported that in Ohio Republic Steel "spies shadowed union organizers; its police attacked and beat them; its superintendents and foremen threatened, laid off and discharged employees for union activities."

SWOC lost its efforts to organize the four "Little Steel" companies in 1937 but victory came later after the LaFollette Committee's exposé, extensive National Labor Relations Board hearings and after some personal damage suits were won.

Republic paid $350,000 to the men who had been beaten by and shot by company thugs during the strike. Some 5,000 fired strikers were restored to their jobs at Republic with back pay of a half-million dollars. Bethlehem was ordered to stop interfering with SWOC. Youngstown Sheet and Tube agreed to reinstate discharged strikers and to pay back wages totalling some $170,000. Inland was directed to bargain with SWOC. A Labor Board election at Bethlehem plants, achieved only after successful strike action, showed overshelming support for SWOC.

Republic, Inland and Youngstown Sheet and Tube did not want a public showdown and agreed to recognize SWOC after a cross-check of union cards. Finally, in 1942, contracts were signed with all four companies. The "Little Steel Strike" had been won.

Something else noteworthy happened in 1942. The union met in convention in Cleveland, Ohio, and on May 22, 1942, the Steel Workers Organizing Committee (SWOC) was dissolved and constitutional birth was given to the United Steelworkers of America.

We had come a long way in the years from 1936 in Pittsburgh, when SWOC was announced, to May of 1942 in Cleveland when we raised our new banners reading "United Steelworkers of America." In those seven years, we had been severely tested. We had survived and had established a firm base from which we would make progress undreamed of by that small band of pioneers who were at that first SWOC meeting in Pittsburgh.

When I look back to 1937, when I was a member of SWOC, and look at that first contract with Carnegie-Illinois, and then look at our Basic Steel settlement of 1974; when I consider what the steelworkers were forced to endure in the early days — the deplorable work-eat-sleep-work life of workers in the 1890's — and contrast this to the benefits our members enjoy today, I am both amazed and proud.

In 1936, average earnings per hour in the Basic Steel Industry were 65.5 cents. The latest figure (August 1975) is $7.34 per hour. When these figures are corrected for price increases over the entire period, they show a purchasing power rise of over 185%.

The Steelworker's "real" wages are protected by a cost-of-living clause today. He had no such protection in 1936. He has an outstanding non-contributory Pension Plan, a benefit that was negligible in 1936. He receives insurance benefits on a non-contributory basis that covers hospitalization, surgical, major medical, sickness and accident, life insurance and other benefits, whereas he had none in 1936. His vacation benefits reach a maximum of 5 weeks after 25 years of service, an Extended Vacation Plan of 13 weeks each 5 years for the senior 50% of the labor force, and an annual Vacation Bonus in addition to each week's regular vacation pay — in contrast to almost no vacation provision in the pre-union period.

Benefits that were not available to him prior to unionization, but which are an integral part of his union contract today, include paid holidays, shift premium pay, supplemental unemployment benefits, in addition to state unemployment compensation when laid off, an Earnings Protection provision, safety and health protection, effective grievance and arbitration machinery, complete seniority protection for layoffs, recalls, promotions, job postings, and transfers, and numerous other benefits which enhance his security on the job, protect his working conditions, and add to his economic well-being.

Steelworkers of today have a right to feel proud and to enjoy a genuine sense of accomplishment. At the beginning, in 1936, we had $500,000 to do an organizing job. The Union's first audit, after its first Constitutional Convention, showed that as of February, 1943, we had a membership of 725,625 and a net worth of $1,774,905.19. The audit of December 31, 1955, showed a membership of 1,200,000 and a net worth of $20,193,835.15. As of December 31, 1974, our general fund totaled almost $32 million, we had a Strike and Defense Fund worth $78 million, and a Building Fund with over $865,000. The International Union net worth at the end of last year was more than $110.5 million.

We have become the largest industrial union in the United States with a membership of 1.4 million members, the largest affiliate of the national AFL-CIO and the largest union in Canada. We are the major union in Basic Steel, and in the aluminum, nonferrous metals, containers and chemical industries.

We play a major role not only in the activities of the American trade union movement but also in the programs and activities of the trade union movement of the free world.

We own our own International Union Headquarters Building in the heart of Pittsburgh's Golden Triangle. Our headquarters office is staffed by professionals and expert technicians in such areas as arbitration, pensions, health insurance, safety and health, economics and industrial engineering. We have our own legal staff.

The amalgamation and growth of unions is, in large part, a reaction to corporate mergers and provides a counterweight to corporate power. We are not, however, interested in bigness for the sake of bigness. The substantial funds in our treasury were not collected out of a mercenary desire to enrich the coffers of the Steelworkers Union. Top priority in the use of these resources goes to defending the social and economic rights of our members.

By insuring that no employer can unilaterally determine our members' fate, union power thus helps wage-earners to maintain their dignity and to achieve economic security. The size of the union strike fund, paradoxical as it may seem, contributes to industrial peace as it encourages company officials to bargain in good faith; it deters them from engaging in the heavy-handed approach of the past, which led to many long and bitter strikes.

Similarly, the expansion of the Steelworkers and the integration of the diverse workforce into one industrial union helps rationalize collective bargaining and the work process, improves communication, contributes to efficiency and avoids the chaos of a situation where each of a hundred skills acts completely independently of one another — which would make coordination of the work process very difficult. Thus in some ways the growth of the Steelworkers Union is of direct benefit to a management which has to run a very complex industrial system. But, above all, our Union continues to use its political and economic power to win a greater measure of social and economic justice for the wage-earner.

Significantly, we practice trade union democracy. We are one of the few unions that elects its officers by secret ballot, in rank and file referendums. Being an organization of human beings, we make mistakes and we admit to them. On balance, though, we believe we have served our members well, our communities well and our Nation well. The record is there for all to see — from Homestead 1892 to Memorial Day 1937 in Chicago to the Steelworkers of 1975.

Collective Bargaining
  Labor Relations in Steel:
  Then and Now

II. The Role of Unions in Our Society

II. The Role of Unions in Our Society

As I related in my first lecture, the early struggles to escape lives of drudgery and wage slavery were necessarily fought at great sacrifice and against tremendous odds. These were basic struggles for the right merely to organize and then for union recognition. These efforts were followed by equally costly struggles for union survival, which finally were culminated by the expansion of trade unions into a reunited labor federation — the AFL-CIO — comprised of 15 million workers. Total union membership throughout the United States approaches 20 million.

The initial goal of workers and their unions was to bargain for benefits that would give them a measure of security and dignity at the workplace. But the union and its members quickly realized the need for involvement in other issues and problems affecting society. It is this aspect that I would now like to examine. In the concluding lecture, I will discuss in detail the relationship that now exists between the Nation's major Basic Steel companies and the United Steelworkers of America.

I have lived a great part of my Union's history and I can say with honest conviction that the United Steelworkers of America — that organized labor as a whole — has played and does play a constructive role in our free society. Labor is an essential part of the fabric of our democratic society.

Basic economic necessity caused unions — from their earliest days — to speak out as a peoples' lobby. In virtually every area of social concern the labor movement has vigorously supported needed legislation. We have, for example, been leading exponents of federal aid to education, the war on poverty, Medicare, higher Social Security benefits, consumer protection, rapid transit, pension security and a national health program. These constitute just a very few of the many, many bills that we have supported in Congress for the common good. No other group in the Nation has concerned itself with, and has so consistently fought for, such a wide-ranging program for social and economic improvement. Nor has any other group contributed more to strengthening our society. This is a proud part of labor history.

We enjoy today a free society but, perhaps, one not yet as free as it should be for all our people. We are considered a free society because freedom and equality are basic, underlying rights that are supposed to be guaranteed to every citizen. Organized labor is working to fulfill that promise. A society is free — and will remain free — if its people have faith in it; have faith that they are getting a fair shake; have faith that they are being listened to; have faith that tomorrow — or the next day — will be better than today. As Oliver Wendell Holmes said, ". . . I find the great thing in this world is not so much where we stand as in what direction we are moving."

Labor has helped Americans keep the faith in our democracy. Organized labor's commitment to human and social progress came early and has been sustained. One of the first legislative objectives of organized labor in America was for free public schools — the universal education of American children as an investment in our future. Unions and workers' parties in the first half of the 19th Century were determined that the promise of our democracy should be fulfilled through equality of opportunity and the uprooting of class privileges. The Workingmen's Party, organized in New York City in 1829, included as one of its principal planks a demand for a school system "that shall unite under the same roof the children of the poor man and the rich, the widow's charge and the orphan, where the road to distinction shall be superior industry, virtue and acquirement without reference to descent."

The U. S. labor movement has never slackened in its close attention to education problems. Like the early unions that preceded it, the American Federation of Labor, from its founding convention in 1881, and the CIO, from its first days, have been champions of the schools, the students and the teachers. Phil Murray, the first and founding President of the Steelworkers, served as a member of the Pittsburgh Board of Education for 24 years. Here was a man whose interest in the best possible education for children was motivated by his own lack of formal education as a child.

As I pointed out earlier, Mr. Murray was forced to go to work in the coal mines of his native Scotland at the age of ten.

The 1955 merger convention of the AFL and the CIO reaffirmed labor's support for the schools. It called for the use of Federal funds for school construction, improved teachers' salaries, health and welfare services for all children, loans and scholarships for all worthy students and the elimination of adult illiteracy. Among the education bills which have been passed by the Congress with active labor support have been the Elementary and Secondary Education Act of 1965, the Higher Education Act of 1965, the "Cold War" GI bill and, of course, many others. Throughout its entire history, organized labor has championed public education. John Dewey, one of the great architects of the American educational system, said of the labor movement, "There is no organization in the United States — I do not care what its nature is — that has such a fine record in the program of liberal progressive education."

Another early objective of the labor movement was the elimination of child labor, not only for humanity's sake but again to give children hope for a better life. Such lofty goals have guided labor throughout its history.

The United Steelworkers of America, and labor in general, know well that the best defense against enemies of our democratic system is to make certain that it is healthy and secured on a sound economic foundation. It is precisely on those grounds that I believe that the United Steelworkers of America, and the rest of the American trade union movement, have made a monumental contribution to strengthening the vital components of the American system.

We are just a few weeks away from the 46th anniversary of that "Black Tuesday" in October that symbolized the onset of the stock market crash and the worst depression in our Nation's history. At the worst of the Depression, there were nearly 13 million workers unemployed and the national unemployment rate stood at nearly 25%. The modern labor movement came into being as a result of that Depression — and much of its economic and social philosophy and many of its programs have been to build defenses against any disastrous repetition. The Depression, which shocked Americans, was a turning point in our history.

I know that the so-called "Great Depression" had its lasting effects on me because I lost my job as a moulder when our foundry was shut down. I was lucky enough later to find a job firing kilns in a brickyard for 16 cents an hour, 12 hours a day, seven days a week. That miserable job led me to re-examine my social thinking; to point me in the direction I was to travel the rest of my life. It taught me that a strong labor movement was essential if a worker was to have any hope of a better tomorrow.

Those years of widespread privation and human suffering taught me and most Americans that such an economic disaster could easily destroy our form of government, our democracy. They taught us that a healthy economy is vital insurance for a free society.

It is a cardinal assumption of labor that economic growth and prosperity are imperative ingredients for a free society — essential elements of democracy; and that the opposite — depression and unemployment — create the sharp tensions and uncertainties which all too often lead to division and suspicion, and foment dangerous actions. We will never forget the lesson of the Great Depression. The kind of social and economic environment in which steelworkers and other workers then lived was not conducive to strengthening their faith in society and the private enterprise system, or the future of either.

What is required for a free society, we have come to learn as our Union progressed and matured, is a degree of economic security for all Americans. In that respect alone, our Union and labor as a whole have been a positive force in helping keep our society free.

Contrary to the opinion of many that unions and union members are interested only in wages and fringe benefits, the record clearly shows that organized labor has been the cutting edge of decent legislation in our Nation. Despite what some critics think it is fashionable to say about labor's stand on issues, we have been first on Capitol Hill in Washington, and in the legislative halls of all our state capitals, promoting a great array of sound social legislation.

Permit me to be specific. After each session of the Congress, the AFL-CIO publishes a report on what the Congress did on the many issues that came before it. The AFL-CIO, of course, takes a stand on, and actively lobbies on, many vital issues. In the 89th Congress, which was the most progressive Congress in history, the AFL-CIO took a stand on 71 pieces of legislation. Only 16 of these could be considered as labor legislation, such as a Federal pay raise and situs picketing. The remainder — a much larger total of 55 — were non-labor bills, such as truth in packaging and home rule for the District of Columbia. The long fight to assure health care for elderly Americans succeeded in the 1965 session of the 89th Congress with the passage of Medicare — an objective of the labor movement for many previous sessions.

The list of other significant pieces of legislation that we supported, and helped pass, or lobbied for in the 89th Congress, is too long to enumerate. But on that list were Medicare and other sweeping Social Security improvements, aid to education at every level, Federal protection of voting rights, a stepped-up war on poverty and a broad regionally-based public works program, a new Department of Housing and Urban Development, a better and stronger housing program, a broad new attack on health problems, highway beautification, immigration reform and a shorter workweek.

We of the AFL-CIO supported those new programs, not because they specifically helped labor unions and union members, but because they were good for the country and good for all the American people. What the 89th Congress accomplished in its two years of existence will enrich the lives of Americans for generations to come. And we of the Steelworkers and labor know that in these struggles our peoples' lobby was essential.

In the 92nd Congress, the AFL-CIO supported 18 issues that could be placed in the category of labor legislation and took positions on 43 other bills not specifically related to labor legislation. The 43 non-labor issues give you another idea of just how broad labor's interest is on issues that we think matter in a free society — National Health Insurance, Veterans Educational Benefits, School Lunch Program, Public Land Management, Public Health Service Hospitals, Equal Rights Amendment, Campaign Reform, Radio Free Europe and the Strategic Arms Limitation Treaty.

In the last Congress — the 93rd Congress — we took positions on 19 pieces of purely labor legislation but were active on behalf of 64 other bills that were not concerned with workers or unions as such. The non-labor issues included 16 programs in the area of health, education and welfare, seven in the area of housing and urban affairs, seven in foreign affairs and eight dealing with consumer protection.

Another example of labor's broad role in our society was demonstrated at our Union's 17th Constitutional Convention last year in Atlantic City. There were 44 resolutions adopted at that convention and many of the resolutions naturally dealt with what could be termed labor issues. But many of them also dealt with other areas of general concern such as civil rights, civil liberties, the environment, energy, world affairs, senior citizens, and the expansion of existing school programs such as Headstart and Upward Bound to meet the special needs of children of disadvantaged families.

President Lyndon Johnson said in 1965: "The AFL-CIO has done more good for the people than any other group in America. It just doesn't try to do something about wages and hours for its own people. It helps young and old and middle-aged. It's interested in education, in housing, in the poverty program and does as much good for millions who never belonged to a union as for its own members. That is my conception of an organization working in the public interest. I've wanted to say this for a long time because I believe the American people ought to know the remarkable contribution which organized labor makes to the promotion of sound legislation."

Looking back further than just recent sessions of Congress, I would say that labor's legislative efforts have been consistently exerted on behalf of the general welfare of all the people and all workers. I already have cited our efforts to eliminate child labor and to provide the best possible education for all regardless of income. Past high points for labor also include the National Labor Relations Act of 1935, more commonly referred to as the Wagner Act and labor's Magna Charta because it gave workers the right to organize and to engage in collective bargaining; minimum wage legislation; comprehensive and expanding social insurance programs including the Social Security Act; unemployment and workers' compensation; the Occupational Safety and Health Act of 1970; the Employment Act of 1946, which we call the Full Employment Act because it committed our Government to utilize all its resources "to promote maximum employment, production and purchasing power" — something we have been trying to get the Government to live up to since the Act was passed, but to no avail; and most recently we were the leading proponents in the successful struggle for legislation to protect and guarantee the retirement benefits of workers covered by private pension programs — the Employee Retirement Income Security Act of 1974.

Labor displays its concern for the general welfare in many more ways other than its legislative and political efforts. It does this through the involvement of union members and officials in a broad range of community and public projects, commissions and boards. Union officials across the land serve on school boards, United Way agencies, university and college boards of trustees and a variety of special issue programs tailored to the specific needs of their communities and states. Today, for example, there are five AFL-CIO representatives on the national board of governors of United Way of America; there are seven full-time AFL-CIO Community Services liaison representatives on the national staff of United Way of America; there are 199 full-time AFL-CIO Community Services-United Way liaison representatives in 155 communities; and there are thousands of union men and women serving as volunteers on the boards and committees of local United Ways.

Our Union feels rightfully proud of the fact also that one of our district directors presides over the governing board of the fourth largest system of higher education in the United States — the 27-campus University of Wisconsin System, with some 140,000 students. He is Bertram McNamara, Director of Steelworkers District 32, with headquarters in Milwaukee. He was recently unanimously elected president of the Board of Regents of the University System. He had been a regent since 1971, and he has been our district director since 1965.

I would also note that long before passage of the Civil Rights Act of 1965, which labor supported, our Union took a stand against discriminatory wage practices in the Steel Industry. We fought against the Industry's practice of paying our members in the South as much as 30 per cent less than it paid our members in the North for comparable work. We succeeded in eliminating this Southern wage differential in 1953, and ever since then the wages have been the same for all jobs, whether the job is in Birmingham, Alabama, or in Homestead, Pennsylvania.

I would also cite labor's role in the Watergate affair; calling it to the attention of the American people; publicizing what Watergate involved in the way of threats to our democratic way of life. The AFL-CIO called for the resignation of former President Nixon in October, 1973, well ahead of any other responsible group·interested in preserving our national integrity. President Nixon resigned on August 8, 1974.

Closer to home in Pittsburgh, the Steelworkers was one of the major institutions behind our city's urban renewal program which transformed an area of industrial slums in the heart of Pittsburgh into a beautiful center to be enjoyed by all its people. It is this kind of project, aptly described as a Renaissance, which we would like to see undertaken in every blighted area of our city, and not only here but in our state and Nation as well. Not only do we believe the job to create a more human environment must be undertaken, but we are sure it can be done from our experiences here.

Additionally, our concern for the welfare of all people and for freedom is not confined to events and circumstances within our Nation's boundaries. Our Union, for example, urged Congress to reinstate our Government's ban against the importation of chrome from Rhodesia where a white racist government shamefully and inhumanely exploits a black majority. We pursued this fight for restoration of the ban despite elaborate efforts by some companies to confuse and divide our members on this issue. The primary issue was one of basic human justice for the blacks of Rhodesia where black miners average less than $50 a month, about one-fourth as much as miners in neighboring Zambia.

One could say that labor's interests and concerns about people and freedom are world-wide. American labor has always regarded a free, democratic and prosperous Europe as indispensable for the preservation of world peace and our national security. The AFL-CIO has, therefore, staunchly supported the Atlantic Alliance and European integration. We have consistently backed U. S. policies to strengthen NATO, and opposed measures that would weaken the defense of Europe. American labor has always been keenly concerned about the plight of the satellite nations in East Europe, has protested against Soviet oppression of the captive peoples, has demanded the right of self-determination for them, and has sought ways and means to alleviate their sufferings.

For about a half century, American labor has consistently and vigorously sought to aid and support the development of democratic forces and institutions, especially bona fide unions, in Latin America. The American Institute for Free

Labor Development, an auxiliary of the AFL-CIO, is beginning its eleventh year of activities aimed at helping the efforts of the workers in Latin America to improve living standards, overcome Communist infiltration and subversion, and develop effective and responsible trade unions.

The African-American Labor Center is another auxiliary of the AFL-CIO and it aids the African labor movements in their efforts to become effective institutions capable of making meaningful contributions to the development of their own countries. To date, more than 200 programs have been undertaken in 36 African countries through the Center's efforts in such areas as leadership and vocational training, workers' education and credit unions.

Labor's concern for a world of order in which peace and democratic principles prevail has extended all the way to the United Nations. Our Union has had a particularly close relationship with U. N. down through the years. On display on a plaque in our International Headquarters Building is the following quotation from a statement by Phil Murray of April 12, 1950: "I believe that the best hope for peace is through a strengthened, active U. N."

The labor movement was the first great, non-governmental group to support the Marshall Plan. We support every governmental program to feed the hungry and rebuild the economies of needy nations. The United Steelworkers and the AFL-CIO ceaselessly attempt to help workers build free trade unions wherever we can.

Arthur Goldberg, who served as the United States ambassador to the U. N., previously was the general counsel of the United Steelworkers and a special counsel for the AFL-CIO. And it was my privilege to be named by President Johnson, in 1967, as an alternate representative to the U.S. delegation at the U.N. We are concerned about the misuse of the U.N. by ill-guided and undemocratic nations. We are confident that the U.N. will soon revert to its original great purposes.

I have not cited two other rather obvious facts about organized labor as a responsible force for progress in our

thirty-nine

society — two facts that are either unnoticed or unappreciated. I refer to labor's acceptance and support of the free enterprise system as the system under which our economy should, and does, function. I also refer to labor's ability to function within our two-party political system.

I know that many of our proposals and positions on legislative and economic issues have been mislabeled — among other things — socialistic, far left, radical, ultra-liberal and, for good measure, communistic. Regardless, I hold to the belief that we of labor do merit some credit for our positions on our Nation's economic and political systems. We do work and seek solutions within the systems. At the same time, we constantly seek to improve their performance. We do not advocate a basically different economic system, and neither do we champion the formation of another political party.

There is a difference between advocating another economic system and demanding — as we do — that the system work for the benefit of all. There is a difference between advocating another political party and demanding — as we do — that the two major political parties "promote the general welfare" instead of catering to special interests.

We of labor do believe that our economic and political systems must be weighed and judged in terms of their effectiveness in working for the benefit of all of the people. They were not intended to serve the few at the expense of the many. As Thomas Jefferson put it so well: ". . . The mass of mankind has not been born with saddles on their backs, nor a favored few booted and spurred, ready to ride them legitimately, by the grace of God." Or as a philosopher stated it: "Man is greater than any economic purpose to which he can be put. He is not a means or an instrument."

Certainly there are ideological differences in what we seek in the legislative arena and what the U. S. Chamber of Commerce seeks. Certainly we look at the profits of the steel companies from a different viewpoint than the owners of U.S. Steel. We weigh the human costs, not just the profit margins. But our battles are always fought within the systems. We want the minimum wage increased above the poverty level. The Chamber of Commerce says doing so will hurt business and cause unemployment. We want more benefits. The steel companies say they can't go that far. On one hand the Congress decides the issue; on the other hand, the issue is joined and resolved at the bargaining table. But again, within the systems. We say let us continue to strive for what we believe is right but let us continue to reach decisions and resolve our differences within the flexible limits of both our economic system and our political system.

This may not come as any news flash but we of the Steelworkers and labor intend to remain a political and economic force in America because we think we are doing some good. Remove the voice, the votes, the numerical strength, the financial strength and the proven social track record of organized labor from America's economic and political life, and the clock would inevitably be turned back. Some of the worst economic and political excesses in America would surface and discover a friendlier climate for survival. Some of the dignity gained for workers and the elderly and the less fortunate would be stripped away, layer by layer. The scales once again would be tilted against the workers.

Who would speak to the conscience of the Congress and the Nation on behalf of the poor and less fortunate Americans? Who would champion the cause of unorganized workers trying to exist on substandard wages? Who would take labor's place in speaking out for the aged or the neglected?

I am not suggesting that we are perfect or that the Steelworkers or the AFL-CIO deserve halos. Any organization of human beings cannot help but commit some errors or encounter failure. But I do say that our over-all thrust has been for the good of this Nation, our communities and our states.

I see the role of the labor movement as one of making sure that we have a steady, unceasing social revolution that gives top priority to the meeds of man — a revolution that erases the seething indignation among minority groups, brings security and dignity to workers, eliminates the fears of old age and meets the expectations of the young. I intend to do everything that I can to see to it that the United Steelworkers of America and the labor movement are out front, demanding this kind of social revolution and that it be carried out in high gear.

Consider the impact that the union structure alone brings to our American concept of democracy. There are in the United States over 150 national and international unions with more than 100,000 local affiliates. These local unions are scattered throughout our nation and are guided by more than a million local officers, committeemen and stewards — trade union activists who comprise the backbone of organized labor. The work of this small army in the day-to-day democratic processes, at the workplaces of America, constitutes a substantial force for good in the operation of our society. The active involvement in our society by unions, in fact, cannot be equalled by any other group in our country.

How do we keep a social revolution going? We do it by political action and political effectiveness. We do it through unity of purpose. We do it by keeping the trade union movement a constructive force for good.

We want a better society in America. We are committed to the endless pursuit of perfection. That is our philosophy. We believe our contributions have increased as our movement has grown stronger. And we believe that the life of every American, and the hopes of every child, are brighter as a result.

Collective Bargaining

Labor Relations in Steel:
Then and Now

III. Today:
Mature Labor-Management Relations

III. Today:
Mature Labor-Management Relations

Forty years ago, the Basic Steel Industry of our country was a place of brutalized relationships. The hallmarks of America's most basic industry 40 years ago were mistrust, suspicion, fear, intimidation, danger, violence, injury and, yes, death — such as occurred in the Memorial Day Massacre in Chicago.

The turbulence of those days is documented in the labor history of the times. They were prologue to the formation of the United Steelworkers of America, and the early years of the Union severely tested the staying power of the membership.

This is the story that I attempted to cover in my first lecture because it is a proud part of the history of our Union and a part of the over-all struggle of organized labor that is unfavorably noted — if noted at all — in some of the books that pass for history books today. In my second lecture I showed that, once organized labor became permanently established, we turned our attention to problems outside the plant gates and began playing a role in society. In this concluding lecture, I will describe how our Union and the major Basic Steel companies have moved from an early, extremely adversary relationship to one of mutual respect and acceptance.

One must know the facts of the past to realize and appreciate the distance that both sides have traveled. What I will discuss in this final lecture is that long, bumpy journey we traveled together, from a time of bitter conflict to a time when both sides finally were able to approach problems of mutual concern with respect for the integrity of the other.

It will be recalled that the antagonisms and violence of the pre-Union days in Basic Steel were softened somewhat on March 2, 1937, when the first Basic Steel contract was signed in Pittsburgh. We were still to experience some rough days in "Little Steel," but the biggest corporation of all had made peace with its workers. That was the beginning of the road, the beginning of sounder labor-management relations between the Steelworkers and Basic Steel.

At least for a while, the contractual road was a smooth one. Prior to the outbreak of World War II, there were agreements reached in 1938 that did not include a wage increase because of recessionary conditions and the Union fought back attempts to cut wages. Our negotiations in 1941 produced a wage increase of 10 cents an hour and some improvement in vacation pay. During World War II, all contract negotiations were governed by emergency laws.

In 1942, the War Labor Board ruled that the Steelworkers were entitled to a general wage increase of 5½ cents an hour, a maintenance of membership provision and union dues check-off. In 1945, an agreement was reached calling for improvements in holiday pay, shift differential premiums and vacation pay but no general pay increase.

In 1946, after the war and after the Steel Industry had reverted from the 48-hour workweek schedule to the 40-hour week, the Union was forced to strike to win a new contract because this reduction in average hours of work resulted in lower monthly earnings while the cost of living continued to increase. The Union pointed to these facts, plus the fact that the steel companies were saving $125 million a year in premium pay alone and were also enjoying good economic health. In a last-minute effort to break the deadlock before a strike deadline of January 14, 1946, President Truman proposed a compromise offer of a wage increase of 18½ cents an hour — about midway between U.S. Steel's offer of 12½ cents and the Union's request of 25 cents. The Union accepted and postponed the strike for one week, to await the reply of U. S. Steel which finally answered with another no.

Thus the largest strike in the Nation's history began one minute after midnight of January 21. As the strike progressed, meetings were held off and on in an effort to reach a settlement. President Truman urged U.S. Steel "on the ground of the public interest, as well as good business, to accept this settlement." But the break was not to come until well into February. On February 15, John A. Stephens, vice president of U.S. Steel, met President Phil Murray in Washington, D.C., and after some negotiating, final agreement on a new contract was reached.

The workers returned to their jobs three days later on February 18. The first strike in Basic Steel was over, 28 days after it began. The settlement included the 18½ cents an hour pay increase that the Union had told President Truman it was willing to accept when he first proposed the figure as a compromise settlement and which U.S. Steel had initially rejected.

Negotiations in the following years peacefully produced a benefit and wage package of about 20 cents an hour in 1947 and a general pay increase of 13 cents an hour in 1948. Three historic contractual gains were also obtained by the Union in 1947 negotiations. Every job in Basic Steel was to be evaluated, and standard hourly rates were to be established for each job classification. Secondly, the principle of severance pay was established. And thirdly, a beginning was made to eliminate Southern wage differentials — a practice under which workers in the South were paid less than was earned on the same job by workers in the North.

Of the new 1947 contract, Phil Murray said, "It reflects a great contribution to the welfare of the Nation and its people. It removes certain elements of doubt concerning the things labor and industry can do to preserve decent, peaceful, honorable relations." The optimism of Phil Murray was short-lived, however.

The Basic Steel settlement of 1948 was for a two-year period but it provided for reopening after one year negotiations on wages and on "social insurance." The primary objective of the Union in the 1949 negotiations was to obtain company-paid pensions. The Union had gone to the U.S. Supreme Court to establish the right to negotiate pensions over the stern opposition of management, which contended that this was not a bargainable issue.

Negotiations opened with U.S. Steel in June but on July 12 — 12 days before the strike deadline — the Union's Wage Policy Committee met for a report on bargaining progress. It was told that U.S. Steel had refused to even discuss pensions or to consider a wage increase. President Truman then proposed a 60-day postponement of any strike to allow time for a fact-finding board to study the pension question and make recommendations.

Both sides accepted, and the Board conducted extensive hearings. The Industry insisted pension plans were "socialistic" and would destroy the free enterprise system. Many newspapers scolded Industry for its indulgence in name calling during the hearings and for its criticisms of a fact-finding procedure to which it had agreed. For example, Clarence B. Randall, president of Inland Steel, told the Board that its proceedings were "complete madness." C.M. White, president of Republic Steel, stated: "We don't like strikes and they are expensive and bad . . . But if that is the way it has to be worked out, why, every strike comes to an end . . . If they think we are wrong, they strike us, see? That is the way this thing should work. It is a hell of a good way to work it."

The fact-finding Board announced its decision on September 11, 1949. It unanimously approved the Union's request that the steel companies negotiate on pensions and social insurance programs, and it concluded that Industry could well afford to finance such programs. To the Union's request for a wage increase, the Board said it was concerned about the "general stability" of the economy and recommended no wage increase "at this time." However, the Industry remained adamant on pensions and after three strike deadline postponements totalling 77 days, Steelworkers began their strike for pensions.

The first break came on October 31, 1949, when Bethlehem Steel agreed to settle. Then came Republic, Jones & Laughlin, Youngstown Sheet and Tube and, finally, on November 11, U.S. Steel agreed to a pension plan. The 42-day strike was over and the Steelworkers had their pension plan.

The first plan provided for a pension at age 65 of a minimum of $100 per month, including Social Security. The 1949 settlement comprised a total package of 8½ cents an

forty-seven

hour and included a pioneering social insurance program for medical care and life insurance.

There was a shooting war going on in Korea during 1950 and 1951 but the two years were relatively peaceful years between the Steelworkers and the Steel Industry. But as 1951 drew to a close, the stage was being set for a bitter dispute that would arouse strong public emotions and involve the President of the United States and the U. S. Supreme Court.

Negotiations for a new steel contract started in November, 1951, and it was the first time in five years that the entire contract would be open for negotiations. The old contract was to expire at the end of 1951 but when there was no movement, President Truman referred the dispute to the Government's Wage Stabilization Board on December 22 and asked the Steelworkers to stay on the job until the Board could hold hearings and submit recommendations for a settlement.

We acceded to the President's request and postponed strike action for 45 days while the Board held its hearings and drew up its recommendations that were made public on March 20, 1952. The recommendations included an hourly wage increase of 17½ cents, six paid holidays, a union shop and vacation improvements.

The Union's Wage Policy Committee voted to accept the recommendations and moved the strike deadline to April 8 to allow reasonable time for negotiations on the basis of the Board's recommendations. But when the deadline came and a strike was imminent because no agreement had been reached, President Truman seized the steel mills to continue production and went on nationwide television and radio to explain his action and to direct some harsh words at the steel companies. I quote several of the President's sentences from that broadcast: "The companies have said, in short, that unless they can get what they want, the Steel Industry will shut down . . . They not only want to raise their prices to cover any wage increases, they want to double their money on the deal."

The companies appealed the seizure of the mills to the courts and on June 2, 1952, the Supreme Court held that the President did not have authority for such action. Freed of their commitment to stay on the job while the mills were under Federal seizure, the workers went on strike. A month later, on July 4, 1952, an agreement was finally reached and the workers returned to the mills the next day with the largest over-all money package ever negotiated: an average wage hike of 16 cents an hour with fringes that put the total gain at 21.1 cents; the union shop, increased holidays, week-end premium pay, better vacations and shift differentials.

Bitterness had been generated during the strike, yet from it were to come some beneficial results. Phil Murray, prior to the 1952 strike, had made some early efforts to create a relationship between the Union and the Industry in which there was a joint recognition of mutual problems and responsibilities. Such efforts had been rebuffed by management but the 1952 strike produced a changed attitude by the Steel Industry.

Benjamin F. Fairless, chairman of the Board of U.S. Steel, made an unprecedented appearance at the meeting of the Union's Wage Policy Committee that approved the 1952 settlement. He made a heartfelt appeal for better understanding between the Union and management. "We must find ways not only to work together but to live together and understand each other's problems," Mr. Fairless told the Steelworkers, and he continued: "We have had our problems and disagreements since the first union contract was signed in 1937. But as I look back over the past 15 years, I certainly would not turn the clock back, even if I could, to the period that I knew in the Steel Industry prior to 1937 . . . We have found ourselves in a very unfortunate position, and one in which I hope we never find ourselves again. I hope," he concluded, "we have no wounds that will not be speedily healed."

It was at this unusual and dramatic meeting that plans were announced for a joint tour of U. S. Steel plants by Phil

Murray and Ben Fairless to help develop better understanding on both sides. But Phil Murray, unfortunately, was not destined to make such a tour. He died of a heart attack on November 9, 1952, in San Francisco.

When David J. McDonald was installed as Murray's successor in 1953, he referred to Phil Murray's earlier efforts to stabilize the relationship between the Union and the major steel firms. He said that the Union and the Industry were developing a degree of cooperation that never existed before.

The joint tour of U. S. Steel plants promised after the 1952 strike became a reality late in 1953 when McDonald and Ben Fairless did visit the firm's plants.

Wage settlements in Basic Steel were reached peacefully in 1953 and 1954, reflecting improved relations. Also the parties in 1955 made further progress toward building better union-management relations when McDonald and Admiral Ben Moreell, chairman of the Board of Jones & Laughlin, jointly toured that company's plants. There was only the slightest strain in that relationship in mid-1955 when an almost negligible strike of 12 hours occurred. But more serious confrontations were to come in 1956 and in 1959.

In 1956, the entire contract was again open for negotiations. With existing contracts due to expire June 30, bargaining was initiated on May 1 with the Big Three — U. S. Steel, Bethlehem and Republic. The companies proposed a five-year contract with meager wage increases, then a contract for four years and four months with a proportionate reduction in benefits. They also wanted to renegotiate the pension program and offered a plan that would not equal benefits then prevailing in our can agreements for another 30 years. The Union's proposals for Sunday premium pay, wage increases and a supplemental unemployment benefit — SUB for short — were virtually denied.

Workers went on strike on July 1 — a strike that would last until July 27 when the Union and the Big Three signed a memorandum of agreement. On August 5, the last of the 12 major companies signed new three-year contracts that included the SUB plan, Sunday premium pay, jury duty pay, increased vacations — which added up to a total hourly package of forty-five cents, the largest wage and fringe package ever negotiated by the Union.

Once again the negotiations ended in good spirits and repeated expressions of hope for future peace. But the realization of such a hope was, once more, to elude the Union and the Industry. For the next round of negotiations, to start in 1959, would write a chapter in Union-Industry negotiating history that would produce the longest and most bitter strike ever.

Bargaining in 1959 for a new settlement began on May 5 with the Union proposing improvements in the old contracts that were to expire at midnight June 30. In the hope of reaching a settlement, the strike deadline was extended until midnight July 14 but management insisted upon a freeze on wages and fringes for one year and drastic revisions in established job practices.

At midnight July 14, a strike began. The Union offered public, private or Government fact-finding to help resolve the differences but the companies refused. In the opinion of our Union, this strike would determine whether the Union would survive or die. The strike continued, week after week. President Eisenhower appointed a Special Board of Inquiry under the Taft-Hartley Act and then he invoked national emergency provisions of the law forcing the workers back to their jobs on November 7, 1959, after 116 days on strike, under the terms of the old contract. Under such action, there would be a so-called "cooling off" period of 80 days while negotiations were to continue.

The NLRB announced that it would conduct a poll from January 11 through January 13 so the workers could vote on the companies' last offer which was made on October 1. The Industry had made some specific proposals on October 1 but it also made the economic offer contingent upon the Union's agreement to virtual elimination of the protection of local working conditions. The Industry offered no wage increase the first year, 6 cents an hour the second year and 6 cents the third year.

At this point, Richard Nixon, then Vice President, and U. S. Secretary of Labor James Mitchell intervened in the dispute. The steel companies finally changed their position and settled all issues on January 4, 1960. The settlement was in the 39-41 cents an hour range and included a non-contributory insurance plan, pension improvements, and the workers' job rights were to continue to be protected under the agreement. The Union, however, was forced to make a costly concession: it gave up a contractual cost-of-living clause. The longest strike in Steel — 116 days — was over. Once again there was the expression of hope for future peace.

The settlement ending the longest strike also established a Human Relations Committee, made up of representatives from the Union and the Industry, to study and recommend solutions for mutual problems. President McDonald said at the time, "Hopefully, as a result of these studies and as a result of the work of this committee, we shall have achieved a goal. That goal is a strike-free industry." McDonald was a sound prophet in one respect. It was to be the last strike in Basic Steel — up to now and at least until 1980.

In negotiations that followed the 1959 debacle, we did enjoy an uninterrupted period of peaceful settlements in Steel. The bargaining years of 1962, 1963, 1965, 1968, 1971, 1974, produced an unprecedented series of contractual advances. It was in these years that our Union won such trail-blazing benefits as: broader Supplemental Unemployment Benefits, a 13-week extended paid vacation every five years for high seniority workers, dental care, unlimited cost-of-living protection, vacation bonuses, outstanding pension programs, including retirement benefits for surviving spouses, thirty-and-out pension privileges, and retirement checks as high as 85 per cent of what a worker earned when actually working.

Not all of these bargaining gains were free of governmental intervention. In 1965 — the first Basic Steel negotiations under my administration — we won substantial pay boosts, doubled the pension benefits and won the right to retire after 30 years of work regardless of age, but only after the White House knocked our heads together.

In our 1968 negotiations, we introduced for the first time the principle of arbitrating contract issues by referring to an outside panel the sticky question of which employees should be covered by incentive pay programs. We won a great many other gains that year, including pay increases and major pension improvements, but of most significance was the fact that both sides agreed to arbitrate a contract dispute.

It should also be noted that our greatest gains in steel negotiations were made only after we revised our Union's collective bargaining approach and established union industry conferences.

As I noted, at the end of the 116-day strike in 1959 hope was expressed that the establishment of the Human Relations Committee would result in a strike-free industry. Although there have been nothing but strike-free settlements since the 1959 strike, it was not because of the establishment of the Human Relations Committee. This was because the Human Relations Committee approach of 1960, as it turned out, was not widely accepted within the Union because some of the bargaining teams believed that their role in negotiations and their right to make collective decisions was being preempted by the Committee. Six years later, the Union established the new Industry Conference concept in collective bargaining that would assure members in their respective industries a direct voice in negotiations affecting them.

The Industry Conference concept was mandated by our 13th Constitutional Convention in 1966. The Convention action was based on recommendations by the Union's International Executive Board following a special study of our collective bargaining procedures.

In changing the old procedure, the Convention approved the continuation of our old Wage Policy Committee but only to formulate the general bargaining goals of the entire membership. It no longer has authority to approve or reject settlements. The Convention in 1966 initially established full-fledged Industry Conferences in four Industries: Basic Steel, Nonferrous Metals, Aluminum and Containers. These Conferences, made up of local union representatives within each Industry, have the authority to adapt the Union's general bargaining policy to its own Industry, to reject or ratify proposed settlements, and to recommend strikes subject to the approval of the membership involved.

Industry Conferences were subsequently established in other jurisdictions of the Union such as Foundries and Forgings and Chemicals and Allied Products. These will be given the authority and responsibilities of the original four policy-making Conferences when industry-wide bargaining is achieved for them. It is hoped that all our Industry Conferences will eventually attain the type of coordinated negotiations and collective bargaining power enjoyed by our major Conferences.

The Industry Conference concept has proven to be very successful, not only because it has produced impressive benefits but also because it gives each member of our Union a greater sense of participation in the collective bargaining that affects him. His local union is directly involved in the negotiations through the personal participation of his local union president.

We seek uniform wages and benefits in our labor agreements so that competition will not be based on exploiting the wage earner but will be based on American genius for making better products with better production techniques. This, indeed, is the essence of truly constructive free enterprise.

In reshaping our bargaining structure, we also took a close look at our labor-management relationship in Basic Steel. Some of us started to pay more attention to something that Phil Murray, our founding president, had written back in 1940.

As chairman of the Steel Workers Organizing Committee, Mr. Murray in 1940 co-authored a book titled, *Organized*

Labor and Production. I would like to quote a few sentences from a chapter in the book called, "Tapping Labor's Brains." This is part of what Murray wrote some 35 years ago:

". . .as management and labor through strong labor unions become more nearly equal in bargaining power, they can either wage war to gain the spoils of production restriction and scarcity prices, or they can together devise improved production practices that increase social income. . .

"Power, wherever it lies," Murray continued, "cannot in the long run be disassociated from responsibility. If the labor movement fails to develop an adequate sense of responsibility for output, the alternative will be increasing tension and bitterness over 'wages, hours and working conditions,' reducing the opportunity for constructive accommodation and community of interest between management and union.

"Speaking generally, the developing attitude of industry toward its personnel may be divided into four phases:

"1. Paternalistic and un-unionized.

"2. The struggle for unionization ending in recognition, collective bargaining and written contract.

"3. A gradual strengthening in contractual relations and continued efforts toward improvement in 'hours, wages and working conditions.'

"4. The beginnings of labor-management collaboration for greater gross productivity in which both may share, thereby affording organized labor the fullest status and widest hearing consistent with unified direction and control of the enterprise.

"During the first three of these phases," Murray concluded, "especially 1 and 2 — a decidedly militaristic type of leadership is dominant. Only as American industry enters the fourth state. . .will there be a demand for labor leaders who are production conscious and who are ready and able to cooperate with management in furthering the common enterprise."

Phil Murray was writing primarily about the development of more mature labor-management relations. What he tried to tell us in 1940 was that both sides sooner or later would face problems of mutual severity and intensity. When confronted with problems of mutual concern, each would have to decide whether to wage war or work together.

As I have noted, we have done our share of waging war with the Basic Steel Industry over the years. But as we fought those bargaining wars down through the years, conditions began to change. Just as Mr. Murray predicted, problems of concern to both sides began to emerge in the Industry in the late 1950's and 1960's.

The world trade scene, for example, had changed drastically and many American Industries and workers were beginning to be affected adversely by an increasing flood of imports, encouraged by the fact that our market was the most wide open market in the world. The American Steel Industry and our Union recognized the import threat and decided jointly to do something about it. At the same time, the Steel Industry was being handicapped somewhat by a low rate of improvement in productivity.

We did something about these twin problems of imports and productivity in our 1971 negotiations by including a provision in the settlement that established a joint advisory committee at each plant to devise means of improving productivity and promoting the use of domestic steel.

Before talking about the details of the contract clause dealing with imports and productivity, I would like to summarize briefly the highlights of our 1971 Basic Steel contract settlement. It produced substantial improvements in every major area of the previous agreements but most significantly it also provided an unlimited cost-of-living clause. The general pay increases over the three years of the contract ranged from 75 cents an hour to $1.15 per hour. The cost-of-living adjustments, including a guaranteed minimum adjustment of 25 cents an hour, were over and above these figures. We also made significant breakthroughs in the pension program by enabling a worker with 30 years of service to retire, regardless of age, with a monthly pension of $255, a $60-a-month increase over the previous contract. We had won the thirty-and-out privilege in 1965. Significant improvements were also negotiated in 1971 to improve hospital and surgical insurance coverage, including physician's charges for emergency treatment in a hospital, clinic or a physician's office.

Now, getting back to the contract clause on productivity and imports, when we agreed to a joint program on productivity we made it very clear that our wages, working conditions, rights and benefits were protected by contract and were not to be jeopardized by the joint productivity effort. In the past, when management talked about increasing productivity, it meant to the workers that management was going to speed up production, or combine jobs, and make layoffs. Productivity became a dirty word to workers. That is why we had to be sure that management had no misconceptions about our role in productivity or the precise purpose of the joint committees on productivity that were to be established.

Management accepted our position and only then could we approach the productivity problem with the right attitude. The result has been that productivity has been increased. This was done through more effective use of equipment, better tools and modern technology, increased worker effectiveness, reducing equipment breakdowns and absenteeism, eliminating waste and the negligent use of materials, using facilities and time more efficiently, improving the plant safety experience, and so forth.

We were able to take this step because we had reached that stage in life — we of the Union and the leaders of the American Steel Industry — where we had developed a mutual understanding and respect. The joint plant committees on productivity were established and started to function, late in 1972 and throughout 1973, with some success. In 1973, the Labor Department announced that steel was the only major Industry that had a significant increase in productivity.

Our 116-day strike in 1959 set the stage for the import problem because it provided foreign steel makers with an initial opportunity to acquire and cultivate American customers. From that time on, imports started to build up each time we went to the bargaining table. During our negotiating periods, the market was glutted with more and more imported steel as a strike hedge. Meanwhile, the Industry would produce more steel to satisfy the stockpiling that steel customers undertook in anticipation of a strike.

That stockpiling process had its impact not only on our bargaining successes at the negotiating table, but it also had a tremendous impact on the ups and downs of production and employment. Our members in Basic Steel were on a "feast and famine" or "boom-bust" treadmill. Long hours of work and lots of overtime were imposed just prior to the negotiating periods and during the negotiating period. But when a contract settlement was reached, the steel stockpiles had to be used up and this brought partial plant shutdowns, costly to the companies, and prolonged layoffs of our members.

In 1967, the Union and the Industry decided we had to do something about solving the twin problems of stockpiling and imports. They were proving too costly to both sides and it was obvious that they had to be solved by mutual action. A search was started for a new way to conduct our negotiations. We thought we had the answer before our 1968 negotiations but we didn't.

Neither were we successful in finding a solution prior to our 1971 negotiations — at which time the "boom-bust" cycle became even worse. In 1971, for the first time, the Steel Industry laid off workers and shut down mills and plants one full month in advance of the expiration date of our contracts and the possible commencement of a strike.

Following the 1971 peaceful settlement, many more production units were shut down. The stockpiling and related problems following those 1971 negotiations cost the 10 largest steelmakers an estimated $80 million in stockpiling costs. Some of our members went jobless for more than seven months because of steel stockpiling that year.

Furthermore, steel imports in 1971 set an all-time high — 18.3 million tons — representing the *export* of at least 108,000 full-time job opportunities in the American Steel Industry. These harsh economic after-effects of the 1971 negotiations spurred both sides on with renewed vigor in search for a new bargaining approach. This time we succeeded by developing an Experimental Negotiating Agreement — ENA for short — a bargaining procedure that was used in last year's steel negotiations.

The Union's 600-member Basic Steel Industry Conference approved the new bargaining approach in March, 1973, and the Union and the Industry issued a joint statement in which we stated:

"Both parties feel sure that the action taken today will assure the Nation and steel customers a constant supply of steel and an end to the 'boom-bust' cycles associated with past labor negotiations...The new agreement not only provides for additional wages and benefits for employees, but will also provide an opportunity for the companies to increase production through stability of operations and enhance the Steel Industry's competitive position."

Briefly, this is what the new bargaining procedure provides: certain guaranteed minimum benefits for our members, such as at least a 3% wage hike each year of the three-year agreement; plus the one-time payment of a $150 bonus because of the savings the companies would realize from avoiding the effects of stockpiling; continuation of our cost-of-living clause without a floor or a ceiling; and elimination of the possibility of an industry-wide strike or lockout.

Aside from a few "sacred cow" matters, such as the union shop, safety and health guarantees and management rights, the ENA enabled the parties to negotiate freely in all economic and fringe benefit areas. And for the first time, it gave our local unions the right to strike over local issues. It provided for the voluntary arbitration of any unresolved bargaining issues.

The new procedure worked. We reached agreement in

1974 on a new three-year settlement that provides our members in the 10 major steel companies with the best contract ever negotiated, and not one bargainable issue had to be submitted to arbitration. And not one of our local unions went on strike over a local issue.

ENA did what the parties intended it to do; it avoided the erratic employment and production cycles that attended crisis bargaining in past years; it eliminated the need to stockpile. In fact, ENA proved so successful in 1974 that both sides agreed to try it again in 1977, thus assuring continued labor-management stability in the 10 companies until at least 1980.

I am proud to note that under the ENA arrangement, in terms of wages and fringe benefits, we emerged with what was generally regarded as the biggest and best settlement of any labor contract negotiated during that period. The 1974 settlement provided general wage increases totaling 60 cents an hour, improved pensions, a cost-of-living adjustment in pension benefits for those retiring under the 1974 settlement, an improved cost-of-living escalator clause to more accurately reflect actual boosts in living costs, medical care insurance for retirees for the first time (until eligible for Medicare), a pre-paid dental program for the first time, a doubling of shift differential premium pay, additional vacation time and larger vacation bonuses, and other gains in such areas as supplemental unemployment benefits and sickness and accident benefits. We successfully reduced the normal retirement age from 65 to 62 with full pensions. The minimum monthly pension benefit payment was raised so that a 30-year employee, who would previously have received a pension of $255, now gets $352.50 monthly under the 1974 settlement, and this does not include Social Security.

It was not only the best settlement in the history of our Union but, in my opinion, we made labor-management history. For the first time, we concluded a complete, major settlement in a critical Industry without the threat of an industry-wide strike or lockout. The new bargaining procedure that we helped pioneer establishes the fact that it is possible to negotiate agreements as effectively as when the traditional weapons of labor and management are present at the bargaining table. This, to me, is a new, revolutionary event in the collective bargaining process.

Some say we gave up the right to strike while the companies have given up nothing. I remind those critics that the companies did give up two precious prerogatives: The right to impose a lockout and the right to take a strike, as they often have done in the past.

This new, revolutionary approach to traditional bargaining procedures may or may not be the complete answer for stabilizing labor-management relations in other industries but it does merit study. This is not just our opinion but it is the opinion of many other observers of the collective bargaining scene.

W. J. Usery, Jr., Director of the Federal Mediation and Conciliation Service, congratulated both the Union and the Industry for what he called their "courage and creativeness." AFL-CIO President George Meany hailed the procedure as "an excellent example of sound collective bargaining and labor-management statesmanship." Secretary of Labor Peter J. Brennan called the Experimental Negotiating Agreement an "historic step." *The New York Times* called the ENA "a breakthrough toward rationality" and added: "The security of American jobs, stability of the dollar and the competitiveness of American products in world markets will all gain if labor and management follow steel's lead in substituting reason for economic force in industrial relations." There were many such editorial comments in newspapers from all sections of the country. They all cited the ENA as a sound hope for future peace in labor-management relations.

I believe that the procedure we used so successfully last year in our Basic Steel negotiations demonstrates that organized labor is willing to join in mutual endeavors that help the growth and development of Industry and also help protect job opportunities. But labor and management can't do it alone. We must have a healthy, viable economy if we expect long-range stability, prosperity and continued progress.

A basic ingredient in providing that kind of an economy is a Government policy designed to promote full employment and eliminate the periodic recessions that sap the strength of the economy.

We believe that the United Steelworkers of America and the leaders of the American Steel Industry — through the ENA — have helped point the way to labor peace in the future. It has been a long road, indeed, from the early, chaotic days in the beginning of our relationship. But we also believe that, at long last, we have reached that stage where we finally have developed the maturity and respect for each other that permitted us to take a bold step of the type advocated 35 years ago by Philip Murray.

In conclusion I again want to express my appreciation for the honor of being chosen this year to deliver the Benjamin F. Fairless lectures and to relate the story of our Union and some of the significance of that story. I also want to express my appreciation to David Brody for his excellent history of the Steelworkers in the non-union era and to the excellent book on the history of the first 20 years of the Steelworkers that was written by Vincent D. Sweeney, who served as the first Public Relations director of our Union. I am indebted to both of these books and authors and to others for their excellent research on the events before and after the founding of the United Steelworkers of America.